UNIVERSAL TRIVIA

Discover a galaxy of trivia questions. Every realm of science and nature is here, from astronomy to plants and from computers to fertilizer. This just might be your chance to fool Mother Nature! And you can start testing yourself against the elements with these sample stumpers:

— What bird can fly backward?
— What does each human have 23 of?
— What has existed for about three and a half billion years?
— What is the common name of an infinite space-time warp?
— What is Africa's "white gold"?
— What is a baby rooster called?
— Who or what is ROY G. BIV?
— Where do the greatest number of tornadoes in the world occur?
— What fruit is a cross between a tangerine and a grapefruit?
— What is the smallest mammal?

For answers to these and more than 1,000 other fascinating questions, keep on reading and surrender yourself to . . .

TRIVIA MANIA!

TRIVIA MANIA
by Xavier Einstein

TRIVIA MANIA has arrived! With enough questions to answer every trivia buff's dreams, TRIVIA MANIA covers it all—from the delightfully obscure to the <u>seemingly obvious</u>. Tickle your fancy, and test your memory!

MOVIES   (1449, $2.50)

TELEVISION   (1450, $2.50)

LITERATURE   (1451, $2.50)

HISTORY AND GEOGRAPHY   (1452, $2.50)

SCIENCE AND NATURE   (1453, $2.50)

SPORTS   (1454, $2.50)

Available wherever paperbacks are sold, or order direct from the Publisher. Send cover price plus 50¢ per copy for mailing and handling to Zebra Books, 475 Park Avenue South, New York, N.Y. 10016. DO NOT SEND CASH!

SCIENCE & NATURE

TRIVIA Mania

XAVIER EINSTEIN

ZEBRA BOOKS
KENSINGTON PUBLISHING CORP.

ZEBRA BOOKS

are published by

Kensington Publishing Corp.
475 Park Avenue South
New York, N.Y. 10016

First printing: June, 1984

Printed in the United States of America

TRIVIA MANIA:
Science & Nature

1) What is the most widely-used herbicide and also one of the world's worst poisons?

2) What is the highest point in the United States?

3) 84% of a raw apple is what substance?

4) Is a light-year a measure of time, speed, distance, or intensity?

5) Which unlucky Apollo lunar landing was canceled after an oxygen tank explosion?

6) By what colorful name is a compound of 2,4,5 T better known?

7) About one-fourth of your bones are located in what part of your body?

8) Besides solid, liquid, and gas, what is the fourth form of matter?

. . . *Answers*

1. Paraquat

2. Mt. McKinley, Alaska

3. Water

4. Distance

5. Apollo 13

6. Agent Orange

7. The foot

8. Plasma

QUESTIONS

9) On what planet does a "year" last only 88 days?

10) What do BTU's measure?

11) What are the two main substances of Earth's atmosphere?

12) A device which would not work on the Moon is:

     a. anemometer
     b. siphon
     c. sphygmamometer
     d. hydrometer.

13) What type of orange is a hybrid between the sweet orange and the tangerine?

14) What human organ is 23 feet long?

15) What is the distinction shared by Marie Curie and Linus Pauling?

16) What is the main artery carrying blood from the heart to the body?

17) What are puffy, cauliflower-like clouds called?

18) What bird can fly backward?

19) What is a frozen river that flows slowly down a valley?

. . . Answers

9. Mercury

10. Heat energy

11. Nitrogen and oxygen

12. b

13. Temple

14. Small intestine

15. They both received two Nobel prizes

16. Aorta

17. Cumulus

18. Hummingbird

19. Glacier

QUESTIONS

20) What is usually the result of seeding with silver iodide?

21) What is the tallest living mammal?

22) What well-known instrument measures radio-activity?

23) What is the name of one of the most primitive land plants, consisting of algae and fungus growing in a mutually helpful association?

24) What heavenly body most greatly influences the tides?

25) Which decimal numerals are not used in the octal numbering system?

26) True or false: Each year, plants use more carbon in photosynthesis than is mined throughout the world.

27) What does a female condor do once every other year?

28) What are the high-speed winds which are at elevations of 20,000 to 40,000 feet?

. . . Answers

20. Rain

21. Giraffe

22. Geiger counter

23. Lichen

24. The Moon

25. 8 and 9

26. True

27. She lays an egg

28. Jet stream

29) Vostak, Antarctica is the coldest spot on earth with a mean temperature (in degrees F) of:

    a. – 72
    b. – 38
    c. – 5
    d. 0

30) What is the dormant state of some animals in nature?

31) What is the main food of baleen whales?

32) What weather phenomenon causes more deaths in the U.S. annually than any other except lightning?

33) What is the dominant sensory modality of human beings?

34) Where is the Great Red Spot?

35) What product does viniculture produce?

36) What does each human have 23 of?

37) Name the type of wood whose normal cells have been replaced with mineral deposits.

38) What dog has short legs, protruding eyes, and was originally bred in China?

. . . Answers

29. a

30. Hibernation

31. Krill

32. Tornadoes

33. Vision

34. Jupiter

35. Wine grapes

36. Chromosome pairs

37. Petrified wood

38. Pekingnese

39) What is the slowest-growing plant, taking 30 years for just one branch to form?

40) What hormone is released during an emergency?

41) What do the numbers 2, 5, 31, and 59 have in common?

42) What is the most popular tuberous root?

43) The Asteroid Belt is between the orbits of which two planets?

44) What cloud formation extends in a long, low layer?

45) Early paper, called papyrus, was made from what?

46) True or false: In right handed people, motor control is ruled by the left half of the brain.

47) What has 1/1800th of the mass yet the same amount of charge as a proton?

48) Ancient Hindu law required surgeons to remove what part of the anatomy as punishment for adultery?

. . . *Answers*

39. Saguaro cactus

40. Adrenaline

41. They are all prime numbers

42. Potato

43. Mars and Jupiter

44. Stratus clouds

45. Papyrus reeds

46. True

47. Electron

48. The nose

49) The use of what material in the Stone Age grew to such a large scale that it eventually had to be mined?

50) What has existed for about three and a half billion years?

TYPES OF PLANT POLLINATION:

51) Pollination by insects.   a. Anemophily.

52) Pollination by birds.   b. Autogamy.

53) Pollination by wind.   c. Entomophily.

54) Self-pollination.   d. Ornithophily.

55) Plants get their nitrogen from:
    a. rain
    b. the soil
    c. the air

56) Rocky Mountain columbine is which state's state flower?

57) What cannot be trisected by classical means?

58) What is the pollen-bearing organ in a flower, made up of a slender stalk and a pollen sac?

. . . *Answers*

49. Flint

50. Life on Earth

51. c

52. d

53. a

54. b

55. b

56. Colorado

57. An angle

58. The stamen

59) The human brain can store up to how many bits of information:
    a. 10 million
    b. 10 billion
    c. 10 trillion
    d. 100 trillion

60) What is a word for the diffusion of fluids thru a semipermeable membrane?

61) True or false: Diamond burns up at 900 degrees C.

62) What burrowing, ant-eating African mammal has a name meaning "earth pig"?

63) True or false: The woodpecker has a sharp tongue with barbs that pulls insects out of cracks in the wood.

64) What is the decimal equivalent of 6/8?

65) What is the better-known name for the deadly poison prussic acid?

66) What percent of the state of California is classified as desert?

67) What colorless, pungent solution is often used as a biological preservative?

. . . Answers

59. d

60. Osmosis

61. True

62. Aardvark

63. True

64. 0.75

65. Cyanide

66. 24 percent

67. Formaldehyde

QUESTIONS

68) What is the common name of an infinite spacetime warp?

69) During what season is the Sun furthest from Earth?

70) What surgical tool cuts without a blade?

71) What is the yellow poplar tree called?

72) Which household device is based on the sexagesimal number system?

73) You would not even like to sail down which New York canal?

74) Which heavenly bodies aside from the Moon exhibit phases?

75) The echinoderm which causes widespread damage to the Great Barrier Reef by eating the coral is:
    a. crown of thorns starfish
    b. sea urchin
    c. sea cucumber

76) What herb was thought to breed scorpions in the Middle Ages?

77) What is the mammal native only to the eucalyptus forests of Australia?

. . . Answers

68. Black hole

69. Summer

70. Laser

71. Tulip tree

72. Clock

73. Love Canal

74. Mercury and Venus

75. a

76. Basil

77. Koala

78) There are 50,000 in China and 26 in the USA. What are they?

79) What is the name of the essential matter of all animal and plant cells whose root word means "first-formed"?

80) What is the common term for an organic catalyst?

81) Name a stubborn hybrid.

82) What do you get when you order sweetbreads in a restaurant?

83) What organ of our body uses 20 percent of all the oxygen we breathe?

84) True or false: An elephant's trunk contains 40,000 muscles - 70 times the number in a human.

85) What are icicle-shaped deposits of carbonate of lime hanging from the roof of a cave called?

86) The bone structure of the whale's flipper resembles the structure of a:
    a. lobster appendage
    b. shark tail
    c. human arm
    d. shark fin

. . . *Answers*

78. Characters in the alphabet

79. Protoplasm

80. Enzyme

81. Mule

82. Thymus gland of the cow

83. The brain

84. True

85. Stalactites

86. c

QUESTIONS

87) An electrical current in a superconducting ring will typically flow unchanged for:
   a. several milliseconds
   b. a second
   c. several weeks
   d. forever

88) True or false: A baseball pitcher could throw a curve ball on the Moon.

89) Unlike most other rodents, the rabbit has how many incisor teeth?

90) The Forget-Me-Not is appropriately the state flower of what state?

91) Which does not belong as a unit of energy:
   a. erg
   b. BTU
   c. Joule
   d. Watt

92) What is the source of the internal heat of the Earth?

93) What lasted for 21 minutes with a gas gun at the end of a tether?

94) What is the material from which most micro-electronic chips are made?

. . . *Answers*

87. d

88. False

89. Four

90. Alaska

91. d

92. Decay of radioactive elements

93. The first space walk

94. Silicon

95) What fish, when threatened, swells with water, shows sharp spines, and frightens enemies as large as tiger sharks?

96) What is the oldest man-made material?

97) What is the name for the disruption of the co-ordinated contractions of the heart muscle?

98) What South American fish can generate hundreds of volts?

99) What is Africa's "white gold"?

100) True or false: Lanolin comes from the fleece of sheep.

NUMBERS OF SIDES OF POLYGONS:

101) Hexagon   a. 5

102) Heptagon   b. 6

103) Nonagon   c. 7

104) Octagon   d. 8

105) Dodecagon   e. 9

106) Pentagon   f. 12

. . . Answers

95. Porcupine fish

96. Glass

97. Fibrillation

98. Electric eel

99. Elephant ivory

100. True

101. b

102. d

103. e

104. d

105. f

106. a

107) What is the name of the instrument which simultaneously records the changes in blood pressure, pulse rate, and respiration?

108) What is another name for high plateau or flat table land with steep sides?

109) What do the terms "ordinate" and "abscissa" refer to?

110) What event in 1982–1983 was the greatest ocean-atmosphere disturbance ever recorded?

111) What herbaceous, poisonous plant of the nightshade family is often shaped like a human torso with legs?

112) Which animal has the largest eyes in proportion to its head?

113) What is spirogyra?

114) What is a deep-drilled well thru which water is forced up by underground pressure?

115) True or false: Nearly 80 percent of fire-related deaths are due to smoke inhalation rather than burns.

116) What was Willis H. Carrier's 1902 invention?

. . . Answers

107. Polygraph

108. Mesa

109. The axes of a graph

110. El Nino

111. Mandrake

112. Tarsier

113. Green algae

114. Artesian well

115. True

116. Air conditioner

117) Who wrote *The Ascent of Man*?

118) What is the largest flying bird?

119) What is the taxonomic classification between Family and Species?

120) What is the name for substances formed at high temperatures by combining quartz, feldspar, and clay?

121) What object weighs three pounds, uses twenty watts of power, and stores one hundred billion bits of information?

122) The heart valves of what porcine animal have often been used for replacements in human hearts?

123) What is a Chinese fruit about the size of an olive which resembles a miniature orange?

124) What is the largest living lizard?

125) What is 25,000 miles per hour on earth, and 5,300 miles per hour on the Moon?

126) Who or what is ROY G. BIV?

127) What astronomical event will make the headlines in 1986?

. . . *Answers*

117. Jacob Bronowski

118. Albatross

119. Genus

120. Ceramics

121. Human brain

122. The pig

123. Kumquat

124. Komodo dragon

125. Escape velocity

126. A mnemonic for the colors in the rainbow

127. Halley's comet

QUESTIONS

128) What device first proved that Earth rotates on its axis?

129) If two adjacent angles form a straight line, their sum in degrees is:
   a. 45
   b. 90
   c. 180
   d. 360

130) What is the simplest fractional equivalent of 0.35?

131) How many nibbles in a byte?

132) How long is a millennium?

133) What three colors form the picture in a color television?

134) To what familiar fruit is the plantain similar?

135) True or false: There are fewer than 3,000 languages spoken today.

136) Which insect has 7,000 separate lenses in its eye?

137) What are Ada, COBOL, and APL?

138) What is the rest mass of a photon?

. . . Answers

128. Foucault pendulum

129. c

130. 7/20

131. Two

132. 1000 years

133. Red, green, and blue

134. Banana

135. False

136. Horsefly

137. Computer languages

138. Zero

139) Which writing device was patented in the late 1800's but finally gained acceptance in the 1940's?

140) What is the name for water made of heavy hydrogen (deuterium) and oxygen?

141) What is a chinook?

142) True or false: It is possible to turn lead into gold.

143) What is known for its 11 year cycle?

144) What is a baby rooster called?

145) True or false: There are seventeen varieties of penguins.

146) Which is the smallest planet?

147) What U.S. President was recognized as a world authority on American game animals?

148) The latest gold rush is in which country:
    a. Africa
    b. Mexico
    c. Alaska
    d. Brazil

149) True or false: In one second, a hydrogen electron travels over 1,000 miles.

. . . Answers

139. Ball-point pen

140. Heavy water

141. A type of wind

142. True

143. The Sun

144. Cockerel

145. True

146. Mercury

147. Theodore Roosevelt

148. d

149. True

150) What is Benjamin Franklin's best-known optical invention?

SCIENTISTS AND THEIR SCIENCES:

151) Louis Pasteur   a. Geology

152) John Dalton   b. Thermodynamics

153) Niels Bohr   c. Psychoanalysis

154) William Herschel   d. Computer science

155) John von Neumann   e. Astronomy

156) Carl Jung   f. Physics

157) Nicholas Carnot   g. Chemistry

158) Alfred Wegener   h. Biology

159) Where would you find Cassiopeia and Ursa Major?

160) What are the cilia?

161) What is an Asian and African wild dog that hunts its food at night?

. . . Answers

150. Bifocals

151. h

152. g

153. f

154. e

155. d

156. c

157. b

158. a

159. In the northern sky

160. Eyelashes

161. Jackal

QUESTIONS

162) What is a highly contagious disease of cloven-hoofed animals:
   a. parotitis
   b. foot and mouth disease
   c. tetanus

163) What is a selenologist?

164) Between 1979 and 1999, which planet is furthest from the Sun?

165) What is the more common term for amplitude modulated broadcast?

166) What is the name of the second stomach of a bird?

167) A flying machine, a diving suit, an alarm clock, and a man-powered armored car are just a few of the ideas of what visionary Italian of the Middle Ages?

168) What is the more common term for light amplification by the stimulated emission of radiation?

169) How many men have walked on the Moon?

170) What is the hexadecimal value of the number 32?

. . . *Answers*

162. b

163. A lunar geologist

164. Neptune

165. AM radio

166. Gizzard

167. Leonardo da Vinci

168. Laser

169. Twelve

170. 20

QUESTIONS

171) What results from the accumulation of pressure in front of an aircraft traveling at the speed of sound?

172) How many notes are in the octave from C to C on the piano?

173) What is the common name for rice wine?

174) The fastest-running terrestrial animal is:
   a. cheetah
   b. lion
   c. man
   d. jaguar

175) Which common food is 97 percent water?

176) What is the name of the plant that was a supposed remedy for rabies?

177) True or false: Kangaroos never drink water.

178) Where do the greatest number of tornadoes in the world occur?

179) The average person has how many pints of blood?

180) Which direction would a compass have pointed 75,000 years ago?

. . . Answers

171. Sonic boom

172. Thirteen (inclusive)

173. Sake

174. a

175. Watermelon

176. Madwort

177. True

178. Central and southeastern United States

179. Ten

180. South

QUESTIONS

181) Which of these is not a likely candidate for a computer terminal display:
    a. liquid crystal display
    b. plasma display
    c. cathode ray display
    d. semaphore display

182) To what do "big bang" and "steady state" refer?

183) In humans, digestion of carbohydrates begins in the:
    a. large intestine
    b. small intestine
    c. stomach
    d. mouth

184) What inflammatory ailment caused by ticks was first noted in Old Lyme, Connecticut in 1975?

185) Bird nest soup is made from the nests of what bird?

186) Fumaroles, whose name means "smoke hole," are found where?

187) What are two people that are monozygotic?

188) What is another name for zero degrees Kelvin?

. . . *Answers*

181. d

182. Theories on the origin of the universe

183. d

184. Lyme disease

185. Swift

186. Near volcanoes

187. Identical twins

188. Absolute zero

QUESTIONS

189) What is the acronym for microwave amplification by stimulated emission of radiation?

190) What can adders do with a log table?

191) Which endangered bird pretends to be hurt to lead an enemy away from its chick?

192) What fruit is a cross between a tangerine and a grapefruit?

193) What tree, mentioned in the Scriptures, is a symbol of power, prosperity, and longevity?

194) What is the lightest of all metals?

195) WQuinith what part of their anatomy do houseflies detect sugar?

196) What is the task of the Glomar Challenger?

197) What device is used for measuring altitude?

198) Where does perhaps half the lead in the American diet originate?

199) Who is Sally K. Ride?

200) The relationship between a human and the fungus that causes athlete's foot is an example of:

    a. predation   c. parasitism

    b. commensalism   d. saprophytism

. . . Answers

189. Maser

190. Multiply

191. Whooping crane

192. Tangelo

193. Cedar

194. Lithium

195. Their feet

196. Deep-sea drilling

197. Altimeter

198. Lead-soldered cans

199. First American woman in space

200. c

QUESTIONS

MEANINGS OF METRIC PREFIXES:

201) Hecto-   a. Thousandth

202) Nano-   b. Millionth

203) Micro-   c. Million

204) Pico-   d. Billionth

205) Milli-   e. Trillionth

206) Giga-   f. Quadrillionth

207) Femto-   g. Quintillionth

208) Atto-   h. Billion

209) Mega-   i. Hundred

210) What is the basic material of pearls?

211) What is the smallest mammal?

212) What sixteen foot long poisonous snake will attack a man or even an elephant without hesitation?

213) What fish is named after the long barbels or feelers near the mouth?

. . . *Answers*

201. i

202. d

203. b

204. e

205. a

206. h

207. f

208. g

209. c

210. Calcium carbonate

211. Flying shrew

212. King Cobra

213. Catfish

214) What shelled reptile is associated with the computer language LOGO?

215) What is the lightest of the noble gases?

216) What wonder drug was used for three years by the Army and Navy before becoming available to the general public in 1944?

217) In what year did Neil Armstrong make his historic walk on the Moon?

218) What is the smallest cell in a human body?

219) What is sometimes the "morning star" and sometimes the "evening star"?

220) What is the name of the ocean whose wind systems cause an almost complete reversal of its circulation?

221) To what animals does the the expression, "Red on black, friend of Jack; red on yellow, dangerous fellow" apply?

222) Which vitamin is called ascorbic acid, meaning "no scurvy?"

223) Where is the saltiest natural lake which is also at the lowest elevation on the face of the earth?

. . . Answers

214. Turtle

215. Helium

216. Penicillin

217. 1969

218. Male sperm

219. Venus

220. Indian Ocean

221. King Snake and Coral Snake respectively

222. Vitamin C

223. The Dead Sea

QUESTIONS

224) Who discovered the polio vaccine?

225) The scarab, worshipped by the Egyptians, is what type of beetle?

226) A megaton is how many times larger than a kiloton?

227) What is the largest living bird that does not fly?

228) Who is the Russian chemist known as the father of the periodic table of the elements, after whom the 101st element was named?

229) What animal native to western China is related to a raccoon and can weigh up to 300 lbs?

230) What is the season in which a southwest wind blows with heavy rains?

231) As you go down into a well, your weight:
    a. increases slightly
    b. decreases slightly
    c. remains exactly the same

232) What human body function can generate speeds up to 100 miles per hour?

233) Thunderstorms occur most-frequently during what time of day?

. . . Answers

224. Dr. Jonas Salk

225. Dung beetle

226. One thousand

227. Ostrich

228. Dmitri Mendeleev

229. Giant Panda

230. Monsoon

231. b

232. Sneezing

233. Mid-afternoon to early evening

234) Of the following, the least likely cause of death is:
    a. smoking
    b. nuclear power
    c. home appliances
    d. hand guns

235) Name the pre-historic flying lizards with 25-foot wing spans and 3-foot beaks.

236) True or false: Hydrogen is always a liquid or gas under all temperatures and pressures.

237) What measure of length, mainly used for sea depths, was originally the breadth of the out-stretched arms?

238) True or false: Crater Lake, in an extinct volcano, is the deepest lake in the U.S.

239) Name the bird that deposits its egg in the nests of other birds.

240) What percent of all the species that have ever existed are now extinct?

241) What are chanterelles, morels, king boletes, and slippery jacks?

242) What does the "2" in H20 stand for?

243) What do both neap and spring refer to?

. . . Answers

234. b

235. Pteranodon

236. False

237. Fathom

238. True

239. Cuckoo

240. 99.999 % are extinct

241. Mushrooms

242. Two hydrogen atoms per molecule

243. Tides

QUESTIONS

244) What invention in about 1450 A.D. revolutionized communication and the world?

245) Name the small fish which stopped the TVA's construction of dams for years.

246) What does the Black Necked ("Spitting") Cobra spit?

247) What is the name for iron coated with zinc?

248) True or false: It takes 6 pounds of coffee beans to yield 1 pound of ground, roasted coffee.

249) What is the distinguishing characteristic of organic chemical substances?

250) What is the name for the disruption of our circadian rhythm as the result of lengthy airplane flights?

PHYSICISTS AND THEIR ASSOCIATION:

251) Millikan   a. Cloud chamber

252) Chadwick   b. Linear accelerator

253) Wilson   c. Oil drop

254) Rutherford   d. Neutron

255) Lawrence   e. Alpha particle

. . . Answers

244. The printing press

245. Snail darter

246. Venom

247. Galvanized iron

248. True

249. They all contain carbon

250. Jet lag

251. c

252. d

253. a

254. e

255. b

QUESTIONS

256) What is the name of the substance from the fourth stomach of a calf, used to curdle milk and make cheese?

257) A hydraulic device for lifting ships over shoals was the only patent ever given to an American president. Who was he?

258) How much sugar does the average American eat in a year?

259) A cloud at ground level is called what?

260) How many VHF television channels are there?

261) How many black notes are on the piano between one C and the next?

262) What is the only true flying mammal?

263) Name two conic sections besides the hyperbola and the parabola.

264) A Russian spacecraft landing on which planet had to penetrate a thick layer of sulfuric acid in its atmosphere?

. . . Answers

256. Rennet

257. Abraham Lincoln

258. 130 pounds

259. Fog

260. 12

261. Five

262. The bat

263. Circle and ellipse

264. Venus

265) What tall, annual plant native to northern Asia yields a strong fiber used for ropes and the drug cannabis:
    a. Himalayan primula
    b. hemp
    c. wild rhubarb
    d. fortunella

266) What snake is responsible for one quarter of all snake bite deaths in India?

267) Who was the first person to be awarded a Nobel prize twice?

268) Sapphires and rubies rank second in hardness to what other substance?

269) What are Drosophila?

270) What are meteors that strike the Earth's surface called?

271) What famous European construction is made of wrought iron?

272) What was the first major publication to have a hologram on its cover?

273) What plant with small blue or white flowers is considered the emblem of faithfulness and friendship?

. . . Answers

265. b

266. Indian Cobra

267. Marie Curie

268. Diamond

269. Fruit flies

270. Meteorites

271. Eiffel Tower

272. National Geographic

273. Forget-me-not

274) What long-haired, heavy-bodied mammal is native to the high regions of Tibet?

275) What is the name of a domesticated South American camel?

276) A typical caterpillar has how many legs?

277) What does the expression "f2.0" represent in photography?

278) Should the dull or the shiny side of aluminum foil around food face outward in order to absorb heat and cook faster?

279) Core, mantle, and crust are subdivisions of what?

280) True or false: It is possible to see stars within the dark part of a crescent moon.

281) What was originally one ten-millionth part of the distance from the equator to the pole of the Earth?

282) What is another name for the gopher plant which yields a milky latex containing hydrocarbons?

283) What food is considered a "brain food" and rightfully is?

. . . Answers

274. Yak

275. Alpaca

276. 16

277. The relative lens opening

278. Dull side out

279. Earth

280. False

281. One meter

282. Gasoline plant

283. Fish

QUESTIONS

284) In the U.S., over half a trillion a year of these "phosphorus on a splint" devices are produced. What are they?

285) What dairy product has been attributed to the longevity of certain groups of people?

286) What is the whale's baleen?

287) What is the fruit of the oak tree?

288) What is Dendrocalamus giganteus?

289) What low calorie sweetener is 180 times sweeter than table sugar?

290) Not conductors yet not insulators; how are silicon and other "solid state" substances classified?

291) What is the hardest substance in the human body?

292) What is the name for the oleoresin and solvent which comes from several species of coniferous trees?

293) A color with a wavelength longer than that of yellow is:
    a. red
    b. blue
    c. violet
    d. green

. . . Answers

284. Matches

285. Yogurt

286. The strainer in its mouth

287. Acorn

288. Giant Bamboo

289. Aspartame

290. Semiconductors

291. Tooth enamel

292. Turpentine

293. a

294) Who wrote the 1968 best-seller "The Double Helix"?

295) Where do penguins live?

296) What was the life span of most dinosaurs?

297) What is the energy associated with motion called?

298) By the age of 60, most people have lost what percent of their taste buds:
    a. 2
    b. 10
    c. 50
    d. 90

299) What is the most dangerous of all sea creatures?

300) Scattering of light produced what obvious effect in our atmosphere?

. . . Answers

294. James D. Watson

295. In or near the Antarctic

296. 100 years

297. Kinetic energy

298. c

299. Killer whale

300. The blue sky

SCIENTISTS' MIDDLE NAMES:

301) Finley Breese	a. Paul _____ Dirac
302) Alva	b. J. _____ Oppenheimer
303) Graham	c. Jean _____ Biot
304) Ada	d. Alexander _____ Bell
305) Clerk	e. Augusta _____ Byron
306) Baptiste	f. James _____ Maxwell
307) Adrien Maurice	g. Thomas _____ Edison
308) Robert	h. Samuel _____ Morse

309) What is the world's largest active volcano?

310) What are tidal waves that surge up rivers from narrow estuaries?

311) The daughter of what Nobel prize winning couple was also part of a Nobel prize winning couple?

312) What was 18 in Greece in 700 BC and 73 in the USA in 1980?

313) What is the earliest-known bird?

. . . Answers

301. h

302. g

303. d

304. e

305. f

306. c

307. a

308. b

309. Mauna Loa, Hawaii

310. Tidal bores

311. The Curies

312. Average life expectancy

313. Archaeopteryx

QUESTIONS

314) What is happening when gastric juices, enzymes, and bacteria are dissolving solid nutriments?

315) What is happening when a Plutonium nucleus separates into two or more smaller nuclei?

316) Who performed the first successful human heart transplant?

317) True or false: Fishes are the most ancient form of vertebrate life.

318) What is the instrument used to separate light into its component wavelengths?

319) When is the sequence of colors in a rainbow reversed?

320) At what temperature is water the densest?

321) How would a person designated as mesomorphic appear?

322) What is the largest crew ever to fly in a U.S. space vehicle?

323) True or false: The proof of the four-color map theorem was the first major mathematical proof performed on a computer.

. . . *Answers*

314. Digestion

315. Fission

316. Dr. Christiaan Barnard

317. True

318. Spectroscope

319. In the outer band of a double rainbow

320. 4 degrees Celsius

321. Athletic or muscular

322. Six

323. True

QUESTIONS

324) What is the compound with a name meaning "green leaf" which gives plants their green color?

325) What weighs over 400 pounds resting on your head?

326) What is the shape of the benzene molecule?

327) What is the name for the new technology whereby a glass fiber carries as much information as hundreds of copper wire circuits?

328) What is the primary flavoring for root beer?

329) If you have items numbered 24 thru 58 consecutively, how many items do you have?

330) What are the front cutting teeth called?

331) What mammal was worshipped by the ancient Egyptians?

332) What is 93 million miles away?

333) What is the term for the apparent shift of stars as viewed from different places in earth's orbit?

334) What part of Earth weighs about 5.7 quadrillion tons?

. . . *Answers*

324. Chlorophyll

325. The atmosphere

326. A ring

327. Fiber optics (opto-electronics)

328. Sassafras

329. 35

330. Incisors

331. Cat

332. The Sun

333. Parallax

334. The atmosphere

QUESTIONS

335) How many letters of the alphabet are identical to their mirror images?

336) True or false: Eggshells, kidney stones, bones, and gypsum are examples of biomineralization.

337) The members of the sub-phyllum Vertebrata have what distinguishing characteristic?

338) What is another name for the mescal cactus, known for its buttons?

339) What instrument records the direction, intensity, and time of earthquakes?

340) True or false: The development of celluloid was the result of attempts to produce better billiard balls.

341) What yellow metal is an alloy of copper and zinc?

342) What is the gait of a horse in which the legs move in lateral pairs?

343) Energy that is stored in a system is called what?

. . . Answers

335. Eleven

336. True

337. A backbone

338. Peyote

339. Seismograph

340. True

341. Brass

342. Single-foot

343. Potential energy

QUESTIONS

344) What bird, worshipped by the Aztecs and Mayas, was thought to be part bird and part serpent?

345) Who is Navy Captain Bruce McCandless?

346) True or false: The sum total of all humans, living or dead, is over thirty times the world's present population.

347) For a given perimeter length, the shape containing the greatest amount of area is the:
    a. circle
    b. square
    c. cycloid
    d. right triangle

348) In what number system does 1 plus 1 equal 10?

349) In general, the organisms that are affected by antibiotics are:
    a. bacteria
    b. viruses
    c. antitoxins
    d. corpuscles

350) Lodestone found in birds, bees, and bacteria probably acts as what device?

. . . Answers

344. Quetzal

345. First human to float freely and unattached in space

346. False

347. a

348. Boolean (base two)

349. a

350. Magnetic compass

QUESTIONS

TAXONOMY OF MAN:

351) Kingdom   a. Homo

352) Phyllum   b. Mammalia

353) Class   c. Vertabrata

354) Order   d. sapiens

355) Family   e. Animal

356) Genus   f. Primate

357) Species   g. Hominidae

358) What houseplant of the lily family has a juice which soothes minor burns?

359) What fish lives and feeds in sea water but spawns in fresh water?

360) True or false: In the Middle Ages, chicken soup was thought to be an aphrodisiac.

361) What is the name of a tusked, wild African hog?

362) What technique is used to show a picture of a human fetus in the womb?

. . . Answers

351. e

352. c

353. b

354. f

355. g

356. a

357. d

358. Aloe

359. Salmon

360. True

361. Wart hog

362. Ultrasound

363) What mineral was an essential component of gunpowder used by musketeers in the Middle Ages:

    a. zeolite
    b. Chile saltpeter
    c. phosphorite

364) True or false: The canals of Mars are probably dry river beds.

365) What is another name for Chinese white cabbage?

366) For what studies did Einstein receive the Nobel prize in physics?

367) The state bird postage stamp of Rhode Island shows what type of chicken?

368) Are dolphins mammals or fish?

369) What is the most abundant organic material on earth?

370) True or false: In one second, a beam of light could travel 20 times the circumference of the earth.

371) What is the term for a butterfly's transformation?

. . . Answers

363. b

364. True

365. Bok choy

366. Photoelectric effect

367. Rhode Island Red

368. Some are mammals and some are fish

369. Cellulose

370. False

371. Metamorphosis

372) True or false: Much of what we know about the surface of Venus is the result of visual observation through telescopes.

373) What is the nominal voltage of most flashlight batteries?

374) Which two planets have days which last longer than their years?

375) Who invented the self-contained underwater breathing apparatus?

376) By what abbreviation is the North American Aerospace Defense Command better known?

377) How many Viking spacecraft have landed on Mars?

378) Boars, barrows, gilts, and shoats refer to what?

379) What is a wave with a crest of foam?

380) After what geophysical occurrence might you see Bishop's Ring around the Sun?

381) What was Archimedes' death-ray by which he set fire to an attacking fleet of Roman ships?

. . . *Answers*

372. False

373. 1.5 Volts

374. Mercury and Venus

375. Jacques Cousteau

376. NORAD

377. Two

378. Pigs

379. Whitecap

380. Volcanic eruption

381. Sunlight reflected by mirrors

382) Which uranium isotope was used in the Hiroshima bomb?

383) A black hole with the mass of the earth would be the size of:
   a. the Sun
   b. the Moon
   c. a bowling ball
   d. a marble

384) What plant can grow 35 inches in one day?

385) A squirrel buries approximately how many bushels of food in preparation for each winter:
   a. 2
   b. 20
   c. 200
   d. 2000

386) What is the more common name for "love apples"?

387) What household heating fuel also powers jet planes?

388) "What goes on four feet, on two feet and three, But the more feet it goes on, the weaker it be?"

. . . Answers

382. U-235

383. d

384. Bamboo

385. b

386. Tomatoes

387. Kerosene

388. Man

389) What physicist, after whom a very important physical constant is named, formulated the quantum theory?

390) True or false: Zygote is the name of the cell produced when two gametes fuse.

391) What musical syllable represents the sixth tone of the diatonic scale?

392) Which is the most common blood group of Caucasian Europeans and Americans?

393) What is another name for Java cotton, used for stuffing mattresses and upholstery?

394) Name an extinct bird that had a hooked bill, short legs, and wings that were useless for flying.

395) An average person in the U.S. will consume how many tons of food in a lifetime?

396) True or false: A comet's tail may point toward the Sun.

397) What insect kills more people world-wide than do all poisonous snakes?

398) What was the first state in 1934 to be completely mapped from the air by a group from Harvard?

... Answers

389. Max Planck

390. True

391. La

392. A

393. Kapok

394. Dodo

395. 50 tons

396. False

397. Honeybees

398. Massachusetts

399) With what objects does the North American Mycological Association deal?

400) What is the point directly opposite the nadir in the sky?

401) How many people have set foot on the Moon?

402) True or false: The crack of a bullwhip results from its tip exceeding the speed of sound.

403) What is a saguaro?

404) What favorite red condiment was based on an Oriental recipe?

405) Who wrote "The Life of the Fly" and "Social Life in the Insect World?"

406) The roadrunner is the state bird of which state?

407) How many manned moon landings have there been?

408) Named after Dorothy's dog in "The Wizard of Oz", what is the acronym for the Totable Tornado Observatory?

. . . *Answers*

399. Mushrooms

400. The zenith

401. Twelve

402. True

403. Giant cactus

404. Ketchup

405. Jean Henri Fabre

406. New Mexico

407. Six

408. TOTO

409) What long-horned whale species is not considered endangered?

410) How many teaspoons are in a tablespoon?

411) What are Callisto and Ganymede?

412) What is the one-celled animal whose name means "first animal"?

413) What is the common name for two adjacent sticks, each bearing a logarithmic scale?

414) What metal, named after the Spanish word for silver, was used by pre-Columbian Indians, and was also worth eight times the price of gold in 1920?

415) True or false: As of 1956, more than ten elementary particles were known.

416) True or false: The ratio of known animal to plant species is roughly 2 to 1.

417) What is the heavenly body Charon?

418) How does a platypus feed its young?

419) How does the temperature of boiling water in Denver compare with that in Los Angeles?

. . . Answers

409. Narwhal

410. Three

411. Two of Jupiter's moons

412. Protozoan

413. Sliderule

414. Platinum

415. False

416. True

417. Pluto's moon

418. With special milk-secreting hairs on its stomach

419. It is less

420) What famous star is in the Little Dipper?

421) What is a dried grape?

422) True or false: The skin of a pig can be successfully grafted onto the human body to repair burns.

423) One form of this common element is among the softest substances known, while another form is one of the hardest. What is it?

424) True or false: Since gravity on the Moon is one-sixth that on earth, a high-jumper who jumps 7 feet on earth could theoretically jump 42 feet on the Moon.

425) What is another name for a wildebeest?

426) The leaves and flowers of this nut tree resemble that of the peach.

427) How many keys are on a piano?

428) What was the sacred Egyptian beetle?

429) What do strangeness, charm, and color all refer to?

430) What is another name for a postmortem examination?

. . . *Answers*

420. North Star

421. Raisin

422. True

423. Carbon

424. False

425. Gnu

426. Almond

427. Eighty-eight

428. Scarab

429. Properties of subatomic particles

430. Autopsy

431) What organ is the female gonad?

432) What is an edible flat seed native to India which is used for oil?

433) Which insect was named in the Middle Ages after the Virgin Mary?

434) At 60 mph, how long would it take to drive to the Sun?

435) Where in space is Cassini's division?

436) What turns blue litmus paper red?

437) What is a horny outgrowth of skin peculiar to birds?

438) What is the smallest accessible point or "picture element" on a computer display called?

439) What is the name of mushroom circles in meadows where fairies supposedly danced at midnight?

440) In 4 billion years, what object will become a consuming red giant?

441) True or false: The dorsal fin is near the belly of a fish.

. . . *Answers*

431. Ovary

432. Sesame

433. Ladybird (Our Lady's Bird)

434. 176 years

435. Between two rings of Saturn

436. Acid

437. Feathers

438. Pixel

439. Fairy rings

440. The Sun

441. False

QUESTIONS

442) This planet's orbit gave proof of the superiority of Einstein's theory of gravity over Newton's:
    a. Mercury
    b. Earth
    c. Mars
    d. Pluto

443) What is the name of a substance which changes the rate of a chemical reaction but itself does not change?

444) What female garment is named after the chemical polymer from which it is made?

445) With what phenomena are the terms epicenter, P-waves, and S-waves associated?

446) Who discovered the method of destroying disease-producing bacteria in beer and milk by heating the liquid properly?

447) What is a light, porous volcanic rock?

448) What carnivorous South American fish attacks in packs?

449) What element, named after the asteroid Pallas which was discovered about the same time, can absorb 900 times its own volume of oxygen?

450) What are the two most visible effects of plate tectonics?

. . . *Answers*

442. a

443. Catalyst

444. Nylons

445. Earthquakes

446. Louis Pasteur

447. Pumice

448. Piranha

449. Palladium

450. Volcanoes and earthquakes

ROOTS OF MATHEMATICAL NAMES:

451) "reunion of broken parts"   a. Arithmetic

452) "calculating pebble"   b. Trigonometry

453) "art of measurement"   c. Calculus

454) "inclined to learn"   d. Geometry

455) "earth measurement"   e. Algebra

456) "triangle measurement"   f. Mathematics

457) What organ in the body heals the fastest?

458) True or false: A U.S. liquid quart is larger than a liter.

459) True or false: Steelhead and rainbow trout are members of the salmon family.

460) RAMs and ROMs are what functional part of a computer?

461) In Einstein's universe, what is the fourth dimension?

. . . Answers

451. e

452. c

453. a

454. f

455. d

456. b

457. The eye

458. False

459. True

460. Memory

461. Time

462) What is the classic meal in North Africa whose main ingredient is semolina cereal?

463) What takes roughly 8 minutes to go from the Sun to the Earth?

464) Which of the following is not an element:
   a. einsteinium
   b. curium
   c. mendelevium
   d. aledium
   c. californium

465) What is the name of the first nuclear-powered aircraft carrier?

466) Goodyear's discovery of adding sulfur to heated rubber is called what?

467) What plant used for medicinal purposes blooms in October?

468) Which substance, named for the island of Cyprus, has been mined for more than 5000 years?

469) What is the process by which plants manufacture their own food?

470) The leaf-cutting ant eats only what type of food?

. . . Answers

462. Couscous

463. Light

464. d

465. Enterprise

466. Vulcanization

467. Witch hazel

468. Copper

469. Photosynthesis

470. Fungus

471) A hollow stone lined with crystals is a:
    a. geode
    b. gneiss
    c. laphid
    d. fumarole

472) True or false: Light is bent by gravity.

473) With what scientific instrument is Van Leeuwenhoek associated?

474) True or false: Life on earth is half over.

475) Which part of an ostrich is 45 feet long?

476) What part of the body has no blood supply but gets its oxygen from the air?

477) What insect gives us shellac?

478) True or false: The knot is a nautical measure of length.

479) True or false: Antifreeze added to a fluid lowers its boiling point.

480) The California Gull is shown on a postage stamp as the state bird of what state?

. . . Answers

471. a

472. True

473. The microscope

474. True

475. Its intestinal tract

476. Cornea of the eye

477. The lac insect

478. False

479. False

480. Utah

481) What two elements besides Mercury and Uranium have names similar to the names of planets?

482) What fleshy root do the Chinese value for medicinal purposes?

483) The average American will consume how much food in a lifetime:
    a. ½ ton
    b. 5 tons
    c. 50 tons
    d. 500 tons

484) True or false: In the earth's core, temperatures reach 9000 degrees F, and pressures reach 3.5 million atmospheres.

485) Which cereal grain alone has over 15,000 varieties?

486) On the average, 20 people a day are killed and 80 more are injured by what natural phenomenon?

487) The first drug made by recombinant DNA techniques is:
    a. penicillin
    b. c-corleus
    c. aspirin
    d. insulin

. . . Answers

481. Neptunium and Plutonium

482. Ginseng

483. c

484. True

485. Rice

486. Lightning

487. d

488) What is the triangle-shaped Greek letter?

489) What is 10 hours on Jupiter and 24-½ hours on Mars?

490) What is the term for sex cell division?

491) What is the common name for the disease which is expected to be eliminated within the next 15 years, also known as rubella?

492) What do photovoltaics do?

493) With what human activity are REM's associated?

494) What is the term for an association between two dissimilar organisms which is beneficial to both?

495) What is the final, stable product of each of the three radioactive decay series?

496) What are giant high-speed waves unleashed by sub-oceanic earthquakes?

497) What blue-blooded, helmet-shaped, nine-eyed crab is a close relative of the spider?

498) Who was the first black American astronaut in space?

. . . Answers

488. Delta

489. One day

490. Meiosis

491. German measles

492. Turn light into electricity

493. Sleep

494. Symbiosis

495. Lead

496. Tsunamis

497. Horseshoe crab

498. Guion S. Bluford

499) What well-named woody plant was used for making arrows?

500) What are the sites at which nerve cells communicate with each other?

AVERAGE LIFESPANS:

501) Hippopotamus	a. 1 day
502) Rattlesnake	b. 5 years
503) Mayfly	c. 20 years
504) Mouse	d. 40 years
505) Elephant	e. 60 years

506) The number of vibrations per second of a typical tuning fork is roughly:
    a. 5
    b. 50
    c. 500
    d. 5000

507) What is the Vostok 1?

508) What feature do only Jupiter, Saturn, and Uranus have in common?

. . . *Answers*

499. Arrowwood

500. Synapses

501. d

502. c

503. a

504. b

505. e

506. c

507. The first manned spacecraft

508. Rings

509) Where did the greatest series of recorded North American earthquakes occur?

510) What are Titan, Rhea, and Dione?

511) Used primarily in fertilizers, which element is never found free in nature even though it makes up 2.4% of the earth's crust?

512) The Romans discovered that volcanic ash and lime react with water to form what hard, solid mass?

513) Americans receive the largest amount of radiation from which of these man-made sources:
    a. buildings
    b. television sets
    c. medical diagnoses
    d. nuclear reactors

514) The 200-inch Mt. Palomar telescope detected in late 1982 which returning celestial object, not seen since its 1910 visit?

515) What natural fabric comes from a goat native to the Himalayan region of China and India?

516) What common flavoring comes from the long slender fruit of a climbing orchid?

517) What two bears are not bears?

. . . *Answers*

509. Mississippi Valley (1811–1812).

510. Moons of Saturn

511. Potassium

512. Cement

513. c

514. Halley's comet

515. Cashmere

516. Vanilla

517. Koala bear and panda bear OR Ursa Major and Ursa Minor

518) What is the name for molten rock which is inside the Earth?

519) What is the largest cell in a human body?

520) What produces 80 billion watts of power from 1 gram of uranium for less than a second?

521) Which planets are never visible at midnight?

522) What is the more common name for sodium chloride?

523) What is the name of an optical illusion in which an oasis appears nearby?

524) If the oceans were drained, what would be the tallest mountain on earth?

525) What substance was the "manna from heaven"?

526) Which of the simple machines is the most recent, of which Archimedes' version is an early example?

527) What element, whose symbol is derived from the Latin for "liquid silver", has been found in Egyptian tombs from 1500 B.C.?

. . . Answers

518. Magma

519. Female ovum

520. Atomic bomb

521. Mercury and Venus

522. Table salt

523. Mirage

524. Hawaii

525. Manna lichen

526. The screw

527. Mercury

QUESTIONS

528) Chicle from the sapodilla tree is the main ingredient of what?

529) What is the outer coat of the cereal grain used in cereals?

530) What is the name of a tornado at sea?

531) What is the name of any variety of substances that destroy certain microorganisms or inhibit their growth?

532) What is the term for being non-malignant?

533) The oxide of what lightweight metal forms corundum, rubies, and sapphires?

534) What is a carbon-copy, so to speak, of another organism?

535) This sedimentary rock was used to build the Pantheon and the Colossium:
    a. marble   c. sandstone
    b. travertine   d. ironstone

536) What can you do with 60 phonemes?

537) Which egg-colored mushroom is prized for its pleasant fruit-like aroma and delicate, peppery flavor:
    a. chanterelle   c. russula
    b. saffron milk cap

. . . Answers

528. Chewing gum

529. Bran

530. Waterspout

531. Antibiotic

532. Benign

533. Aluminum

534. Clone

535. b

536. Pronounce every word in the English language

537. a

538) What are the two main causes of acid rain?

539) What is an LRV on the Moon?

540) What animal has the largest brain?

541) What are the three forms of matter?

542) True or false: There are at least 100,000 species of butterflies.

543) What is the most common cause of death among Americans between the ages of 1 and 38?

544) True or false: The average meteor is no larger than a grain of sand.

545) What is the deadliest man-made chemical compound?

546) What is the more common name for Legionella pneumophila?

547) The path of a cannon ball fired from a cannon is a:
   a. semi-circle   c. parabola
   b. ellipse   d. catenary

548) An ounce of what metal can be beaten into such a thin film that it would cover 100 square feet?

. . . *Answers*

538. Factories and automobiles

539. Lunar Roving Vehicle

540. Blue whale

541. Solid, liquid, and gas

542. True

543. Accidents

544. True

545. Dioxin

546. Legionnaire's disease

547. c

548. Gold

549) What does EVA stand for?

550) What is the abbreviation for "deoxyribonu-cleic acid"?

SYMBOLS OF CHEMICAL ELEMENTS:

551) Tungsten   a. K

552) Tin   b. Au

553) Sodium   c. Ag

554) Iron   d. Sb

555) Silver   e. Cu

556) Gold   f. W

557) Potassium   g. Sn

558) Mercury   h. Hg

559) Antimony   i. Fe

560) Copper   j. Na

561) What comes from the dried seeds of the cacao tree?

. . . Answers

549. Extra-vehicular activity

550. DNA

551. f

552. g

553. j

554. i

555. c

556. b

557. a

558. h

559. d

560. e

561. Chocolate

562) True or false: The tuatara, crocodile, and turtle are prehistoric reptiles still alive today.

563) True or false: A single laser blast can concentrate more power than the entire amount of electrical energy being generated during the same time.

564) What is palynology?

565) With what man is the concept of natural selection associated?

566) What is a better-known name for nitrous oxide?

567) What is the logarithm base ten of one thousand?

568) What is the goat antelope whose skin is used to clean automobiles?

569) What human organ expands five hundred times during pregnancy?

570) What fake pills can sometimes relieve symptoms?

571) What whale's name is derived from words meaning "whale corpse"?

. . . Answers

562. True

563. True

564. The study of fossil pollen

565. Charles Darwin

566. Laughing gas

567. Three

568. Chamois

569. The uterus

570. Placebos

571. Narwhal

572) What is a Tridacna?

573) True or false: Contact lenses were introduced in the late 1800's.

574) What ingredient is used for explosives and for heart medicines?

575) What is the mass in grams of one cubic centimeter of water?

576) To what triangle does the Pythagorean Theorem apply?

577) What is the term for an animal that is functionally active at night?

578) With what are TTL, LSTTL, and ECL associated?

579) What is the more common name for the African lemur Galago?

580) True or false: There are more than a million distinct sorts of animals that exist or have existed.

581) With what are the meatus, the pinna, and the cochlea associated?

582) On what planet is the sky red and the sunset blue?

. . . Answers

572. The largest bivalve mollusk

573. True

574. Nitroglycerin

575. One gram

576. Right triangle

577. Nocturnal

578. Electronic integrated circuits

579. Bush baby

580. True

581. The ear

582. Mars

QUESTIONS

583) Whose paradox asks why the sky is not ablaze with starlight if the universe is infinite in extent and uniformly filled with stars:
    a. Olber's
    b. Greigheim's
    c. Schuller's
    d. Miller's

584) Humans are continuously bombarded with ionizing radiation from:
    a. cosmic rays
    b. the earth's crust
    c. radioactive isotopes within the body
    d. all of these

585) What is the third planet from the Sun?

586) What is the major greenhouse flower crop in the U.S.?

587) What state in the U.S. has the smallest West longitude?

588) What is the common name for dichloro-diphenyltrichloroethane?

589) What are the four primary tastes of the tongue?

590) True or false: The largest egg laid by a bird is from the ostrich.

. . . Answers

583. a

584. d

585. Earth

586. Rose

587. Maine

588. DDT

589. Sweet, sour, bitter, salty

590. True

QUESTIONS

591) The first metal to be used by prehistoric man for non-ornamental purposes was:
    a. bronze
    b. copper
    c. tin
    d. gold

592) According to Boyle's law, doubling the pressure on a gas does what to its volume?

593) What is a soft rennet cheese known for its very strong odor and taste?

594) How many millimeters are in a kilometer?

595) In which US state do the most bald eagles live?

596) What is a repeating reflection of sound from a surface?

597) What medical technique involves 800 points arranged along 14 lines running from head to foot?

598) True or false: Our atmosphere has lasted for more than half of the earth's lifetime.

599) Which well-known disease was eradicated globally in 1980?

600) When could you see Bailey's Beads?

. . . Answers

591. b

592. Halves it

593. Limburger

594. One million

595. Alaska

596. Echo

597. Acupuncture

598. False

599. Smallpox

600. During a total solar eclipse

ORBITAL TYPES:

601) Heliocentric   a. Around the Moon

602) Geocentric   b. Around Jupiter

603) Selenocentric   c. Around the Earth

604) Joveocentric   d. Around the Sun

605) It takes light four years to reach us from what object?

606) As you go up to a mountain top, your weight:
    a. increases slightly
    b. decreases slightly
    c. remains exactly the same.

607) How much does a human adult's skin weigh?

608) What animal falls down and plays dead?

609) What is the sum of the angles in a triangle?

610) How many strings are on a standard guitar?

611) What is a culinary term for a raw fish?

612) What is the state bird of New Hampshire which resembles a sparrow dipped in cranberry juice?

. . . Answers

601. d

602. c

603. a

604. b

605. The closest star outside the solar system (Alpha Centauri).

606. b

607. Six pounds

608. Opossum

609. 180 degrees

610. Six

611. Sushi

612. Purple finch

613) True or false: An aneurysm is a bulge of dead heart muscle.

614) True or false? Most singing birds are female.

615) The Hibiscus is which state's state flower?

616) The Dewar flask was the fore-runner of what household object?

617) Which vitamin is called tocopherol, meaning "to bear children"?

618) True or false: Scientists periodically bounce a laser beam off of a mirror on the Moon to measure the Moon's distance from earth.

619) What is the name of an armored, burrowing mammal?

620) Transpiration in plant is:
   a. the process in which plants make their own food
   b. evaporation of water from the leaves
   c. spreading of the root system

621) The root of which plant is used as a substitute or addition to coffee:
   a. chickory
   b. yarrow
   c. sweet woodruff

. . . *Answers*

613. True

614. False

615. Hawaii

616. Thermos bottle

617. Vitamin E

618. True

619. Armadillo

620. b

621. a

622) What scaly anteater is able to roll itself into a ball when attacked?

623) What is it of which a child has 20 and an adult has 32?

624) In the human body, which lung is larger, left or right?

625) True or false: Fireballs can be produced by swamp gas ignited by spontaneous combustion.

626) What plant is a partial parasite that grows in the branches of trees:
    a. sundew
    b. venus flytrap
    c. mistletoe

627) What is the name of a line which connects two points of a circle and passes through its center?

628) What is the brightest star in the constellation Centaurus?

629) True or false: The cones in the eye are responsible for color vision.

630) What are the fleshy appendages on the chin or throat of a bird called?

631) What are QWERTY and Dvorak?

. . . Answers

622. Pangolin

623. Teeth

624. Right

625. True

626. c

627. Diameter

628. Alpha Centauri

629. True

630. Wattles

631. Typewriter keyboards

632) How many degrees is the average human's field of vision?

633) How many gallons of blood are filtered by the kidneys each day?

634) What is the state flower of Florida?

635) What layer of the atmosphere derives its name from the Greek word meaning "I smell"?

636) What is the more famous name for sturgeon eggs?

637) The pecan nut comes from what tree:
   a. hickory
   b. magnolia
   c. maple

638) What is the subatomic particle whose name means "little neutron" which can pass through the earth without a collision?

639) What is any line segment extending from the center to the periphery of a circle?

640) True or false: Triton, Neptune's moon, has an ocean made of liquid nitrogen.

. . . Answers

632. One hundred eighty degrees

633. 500

634. Orange blossom

635. Ozone

636. Caviar

637. a

638. Neutrino

639. Radius

640. True

641) What is 13 days for a possum and 624 days for an Indian elephant?

642) To what note are the top and bottom strings on a guitar tuned?

643) What is the opposite of aphelion?

644) What is a hard, unmalleable iron containing a large amount of carbon?

645) The Age of Plastics began in 1907 when Leo Baekeland produced what synthetic resin?

646) Name the structure by means of which substances of respiration and nutrition pass between the mother and the developing embryo.

647) Which river carries as much water in a day as the Thames carries in a year?

648) Most people need it as children, but 80% of the world's population reacts adversely to what substance?

649) In what number base does $1 + 2 = 10$?

650) What is the term for the old belief that frogs could originate from mud and maggots from decaying food?

. . . Answers

641. The gestation period

642. E

643. Perihelion

644. Cast iron

645. Bakelite

646. Placenta

647. Amazon

648. Milk

649. Base 3

650. Spontaneous generation

NUMBERS OF KNOWN PLANETARY MOONS:

651) Mars   a. 0

652) Uranus   b. 1

653) Jupiter   c. 2

654) Pluto   d. 5

655) Venus   e. 16

656) What disease, spread by the bite of the anopheles mosquito, has a name meaning "bad air"?

657) Who is Louise Joy Brown, born 1978 in England?

658) What is tofu?

659) What is the steady, hot, oppressive wind which blows from the Libyan deserts into southern Europe?

660) What are Diplodocus and Pteranodon?

661) What is the longest and strongest bone in the body?

. . . Answers

651. c

652. d

653. e

654. b

655. a

656. Malaria

657. The first "test-tube baby"

658. Soy bean curd

659. Sirocco

660. Dinosaurs

661. Femur

QUESTIONS

662) During what phase of the Moon can a total eclipse of the Moon occur?

663) True or false: Stars twinkle because of air turbulence due to uneven heat distribution.

664) What is the name of the cord of great toughness, made from sheep intestines, and used for violin strings?

665) What is the term for a state of resistance to an infection?

666) What is the name for a sloping pile of rocks at the foot of a cliff?

667) True or false: A jet plane gains about one pound of weight in flight because of relativistic effects.

668) Saprophytes are:
   a. roots with nodules
   b. flowering plants
   c. organisms that live on dead plant and animal tissue.

. . . Answers

662. Full Moon

663. True

664. Catgut

665. Immunity

666. Talus slope

667. False

668. c

669) Which does not belong in a list of elements:
   a. absydian
   b. antimony
   c. cerium
   d. dysprosium

670) What is the legless larva of the housefly called?

671) What five-ounce baby was suffocated when its 260 lb. mother accidentally rolled onto it?

672) True or false: A millipede really has 1000 legs.

673) The state flower of which state, appropriately, is the Mayflower?

674) Which primitive fish feeds by sucking food from the water bottom and is known for its roe:
   a. sturgeon
   b. catfish
   c. skate
   d. flounder

675) What temperature scale denotes 0 degrees as the freezing point and 100 degrees as the boiling point of water?

676) What are Schmidt, Cassegrainian, and Galilean examples of?

. . . *Answers*

669. a

670. Maggot

671. Giant panda

672. False

673. Massachusetts

674. a

675. Celsius (centigrade)

676. Telescopes

QUESTIONS

677) What body part was discovered by Gabriel Fallopius?

678) What neutral subatomic particle has about the same mass as the proton?

679) How many permutations of four objects are there?

680) What is the distinguishing characteristic of igneous rocks?

681) What is the more common name for the aurora borealis?

682) Who traditionally was the first to be hit on the head with the concept of gravitation?

683) True or false: There are fewer than 200,000 types of plants.

684) What is an area of wet, soggy ground or bog?

685) What animal is a domesticated breed of the wild polecat?

686) True or false: In a geosynchronous orbit, a satellite appears to remain stationary above the earth.

. . . *Answers*

677. Fallopian tubes

678. Neutron

679. Twenty-four

680. They cooled from a molten state

681. Northern lights

682. Sir Isaac Newton

683. False

684. Mire

685. Ferret

686. True

687) What is meant by the statement that an animal is oviparous?

688) What is a better-known name for 'quasi-stellar object'?

689) What is the first element discovered by Mme. Curie which is named after her native country?

690) What is the lifespan of a trout?

691) What are the hormones that control a number of bodily metabolic functions:
    a. steroids
    b. oxytocins
    c. androsterones
    d. cyclamates

692) What mammal lays eggs?

693) The apparent diameter of the Moon is the same as the apparent diameter of what other heavenly body?

694) With what substance are "percussion flaking" and "pressure flaking" associated?

695) What South American country was named after a tree?

696) What was the longest dinosaur?

. . . Answers

687. It lays eggs

688. Quasar

689. Polonium

690. Four years

691. a

692. Platypus

693. The Sun

694. Flint

695. Brazil

696. Diplodocus

QUESTIONS

697) If a neutral iron atom has 26 protons, how many electrons does it have?

698) What is found on Kitt Peak?

699) What is happening when two Hydrogen nuclei combine to form a Helium nucleus?

700) What is the name of the boundary in the mountains above which trees do not grow?

UNITS OF MEASURE PERSONIFIED:

701) (Hans) Oersted,
    (Frederich) Gauss   a. Relative speed

702) (Wilhelm) Weber,
    (James) Maxwell   b. Conductance

703) (William) Gilbert,   c. Magnetic field
    (Andre-Marie) Ampere   strength

704) (Ernst) Mach   d. Magnetic flux

705) (Ernst) Siemens   e. Temperature

706) (Anders) Celsius   f. Electrical current

707) What broadcast band ranges from 88 to 108 megahertz?

. . . Answers

697. 26

698. Telescopes of the National Observatory

699. Fusion

700. Timber line

701. c

702. d

703. f

704. a

705. b

706. e

707. FM radio

708) What is the name of the rounded lateral projection on each bone of the leg at the ankle?

709) What bird has been measured to fly 106 miles per hour?

710) What is the structure inside trees which keeps them straight?

711) What event in 1980 took 60 lives and destroyed more than 150 square miles in the United States?

712) True or false: Light travels the same speed in air as in glass.

713) What substance, unlike almost all other substances on Earth, expands when frozen?

714) What is the class of rocks that were formed in layers under water?

715) Where do alpestrine plants grow?

716) What tropical American tree produces the lightest wood known?

717) What is the name of an extinct, long-tusked mammal that resembled an elephant?

. . . Answers

708. Malleolus

709. Spine-tailed swift

710. Lignin

711. Eruption of Mt. St. Helens

712. False

713. Water

714. Sedimentary rocks

715. On mountains

716. Balsa

717. Mastodon

QUESTIONS

718) In which space program did pairs of Americans fly?

719) Linseed oil comes from what plant?

720) What is the South American beast of burden?

721) True or false: Poison oak and poison sumac belong to the cashew family.

722) True or false: Saturn, Jupiter, and Neptune each has a moon larger than the planet Mercury.

723) During the Bronze Age, what were the only sources for iron?

724) What is the basic unit of heredity named after the Greek word for "race"?

725) What is the costliest man-made element on earth?

726) What is cement mixed with sand and water?

727) A ruby rod is the heart of what recent invention?

728) What is the name of the first atomic-powered submarine?

. . . Answers

718. Gemini

719. Flax

720. Llama

721. True

722. True

723. Meteorites

724. Gene

725. Californium ($1 billion per gram)

726. Concrete

727. Laser

728. Nautilus

QUESTIONS

729) True or false: The Sun has more than 99 percent of the total mass in the solar system.

730) What is a unit of luminous flux?

731) What is the greatest depth that has been drilled into the Earth's surface: 5, 50, or 500 miles?

732) Which planet is Earth's twin size-wise?

733) What is the process whereby a solid, such as dry ice, changes directly into a gas?

734) What starchy substance comes from the bitter root of the cassave plant and is used to thicken soups and puddings:
    a. gelatin
    b. pectin
    c. tapioca

735) What is the name of an annual herb whose ripened seeds are regarded as a cereal crop?

736) What accounts for 75 percent of all living things?

737) What is the decimal value of the binary number 101?

738) What is the name of the interaction of the Earth's magnetic field with the wind of electrically-charged particles from the Sun?

. . . Answers

729. True

730. Lumen

731. 5 miles

732. Venus

733. Sublimation

734. c

735. Buckwheat

736. Bacteria

737. Five

738. The aurora

QUESTIONS

739) What phenomenon has been observed on Io which was previously only seen on Earth?

740) Bees must collect nectar from this many flowers to make 1 pound of honey-comb:
    a. 10 thousand
    b. 2 million
    c. 20 million
    d. 50 million

741) What number represents the ratio of speed of an object to the speed of sound in the surrounding air?

742) For what exactly is John Audubon famous?

743) How many bytes in 1K bytes of RAM?

744) Three is close. Twenty-two sevenths is better yet. What is it?

745) What is the name of the largest terrestrial rodent, distinguished by its spiny covering?

746) What is the term for a line originating outside a circle which touches it at only one point?

747) What is the recollection of past events, or the performance of previously-learned skills?

. . . *Answers*

739. Active volcanoes

740. b

741. Mach number

742. His 435 paintings of birds

743. 1024

744. Pi

745. Porcupine

746. Tangent

747. Memory

748) What is a transformation, often involving yeast, whose name is derived from a word meaning "to boil"?

749) In proportion to its size, what insect has the largest brain of any creature on Earth?

750) What is MCMLXXXIV?

BOOKS AND AUTHORS:

751) *Elements*   a. Darwin

752) *de Revolutionibus*   b. Newton

753) *Origin of the Species*   c. Copernicus

754) *Principia*   d. Carson

755) *Principia Mathematica*   e. Thomas

756) *Silent Spring*   f. Whitehead & Russell

757) *The Lives of a Cell*   g. Euclid

758) Three p.m. Greenwich Mean Time is what standard time in Los Angeles?

759) What is a more common name for EVA in space?

. . . Answers

748. Fermentation

749. The ant

750. 1984

751. g

752. c

753. a

754. b

755. f

756. d

757. e

758. Seven a.m.

759. Space walk

760) The Rh factor was named after what animal?

761) True or false: The nose humidifies and filters more than 500 cubic feet of air a day.

762) What is another name for the plant Deadly Nightshade which women in Roman times used as an eyeshadow?

763) What does a venturi measure?

764) Albacore is a type of:
   a. shell-fish
   b. tuna
   c. marble
   d. meteroid

765) The bark of what tree was used as a defense against malaria:
   a. beech
   b. oak
   c. cinchona
   d. elm

766) What state in the U.S. has the smallest North latitude?

767) How many calories are in a glass of whole milk?

768) What are PVC and ABS?

. . . Answers

760. Rhesus monkey

761. True

762. Bella donna

763. Rate of flow

764. b

765. c

766. Hawaii

767. 150

768. Types of plastic

769) True or false: Carbon, the basic substance of life, makes up only about 0.3 percent of the earth's crust?

770) It takes 17 of them to smile, 43 of them to frown. What are they?

771) How long is a baby kangaroo at birth?

772) Who wrote the Principia?

773) What is the term for people who study volcanoes?

774) Schockley, Brattain, and Bardeen won a Nobel prize for what small invention?

775) Middle-C on the piano has a frequency in cycles per second of:
    a. 20
    b. 256
    c. 2520
    d. 25200

776) In the U.S. twins occur in 1 out of every:
    a. 10
    b. 50
    c. 90
    d. 220 pregnancies

. . . Answers

769. True

770. Facial muscles

771. One inch

772. Sir Isaac Newton

773. Volcanologists

774. The transistor

775. b

776. c

777) The only species of cat that lives and hunts in groups is:
    a. lion
    b. leopard
    c. jaguar
    d. cougar

778) How is the number 14 represented in the hexadecimal system?

779) The most pollution-free source of energy is:
    a. natural gas
    b. coal
    c. nuclear
    d. solar

780) Dentine is the primary substance of what part of the body?

781) True or false: The return of Halley's comet in 1759 was predicted by Edmund Halley in 1705.

782) Chemical substances which end in "ase" are known as:
    a. carbohydrates
    b. sugars
    c. enzymes
    d. glycerols

783) Linen is made from what plant?

. . . Answers

777. a

778. E

779. d

780. The tooth

781. True

782. c

783. Flax

784) What type of coral has a rounded, convoluted mass?

785) What event followed this frantic warning, "Vancouver, Vancouver, this is it!"?

786) The most widely-varied group of vascular plants is:
    a. trees
    b. grasses
    c. flowers

787) A cavity containing a magnetron device, directing waves from an antenna to a waveguide and a stirrer which disperses them describes what home appliance?.

788) With what characteristic of Earth is the value 23 ½ degrees associated?

789) What belts are composed of charged particles surrounding Earth?

790) What is the term for the adjustment of living matter to its environment?

791) Name a tall, flightless Australian running bird.

792) When does the next millennium begin?

. . . *Answers*

784. Brain coral

785. Eruption of Mt. St. Helens

786. b

787. Microwave oven

788. The angle of tilt of its axis

789. Van Allen Belts

790. Adaptation

791. Emu

792. 2000 A.D.

QUESTIONS

793) What phenomenon turns red light into blue and low notes into high (or vice versa)?

794) True or false: The hummingbird goes into hibernation every night.

795) What are the two bright spots of light on opposite sides of a halo around the Sun called?

796) True or false: Men have more blood than women, and it is richer in red blood cells

797) What is characteristic of clouds with "nimbus" in their names?

798) What triangle has 3 equal sides?

799) What is the common name of pneumoconiosis silicosis?

800) Which two planets have overlapping orbits?

801) What mammal is 6 feet tall when born?

802) What do the 1981 headlines 'Copernicus dies, Einstein revives' refer to?

803) True or false: The human brain is roughly 80 percent water.

. . . Answers

793. Doppler shift

794. True

795. Sun dogs

796. True

797. They produce precipitation

798. Equilateral

799. Black lung disease

800. Neptune and Pluto

801. Satellites

802. Giraffe

803. True

804) On what explosive discoveries were Alfred Nobel's fortunes made?

805) The petals of which plant, if eaten by cows and goats, will turn their milk red:
    a. lady's mantle
    b. fireweed
    c. common St. John's wort

806) What has a 30,000 square inch circular surface, weighs 15 tons, and has a polished surface coated with just one ounce of aluminum?

807) What is the name of the body's well-publicized anti-viral agent used in cancer research?

808) What is an area of sunken land which appears suddenly due to faulty subsoil and consumes houses and cars?

809) What is arachnology?

810) What is the resistance offered to the motion of one portion of matter on another?

811) What is the name of David Bushnell's 18th century, man-powered submarine?

812) What prestigious company manufactured engines used in the Concorde supersonic airplane?

. . . *Answers*

804. Dynamite

805. c

806. The Mt. Palomar 200 inch mirror

807. Interferon

808. Sinkhole

809. Study of spiders

810. Friction

811. Bushnell's Turtle

812. Rolls Royce

QUESTIONS

813) What is the largest crustacean?

814) What was most significant about the Apollo 11 flight?

815) What structure contains the vocal cords?

816) Which state goes through 180 degrees West longitude?

817) What satellite carried the first live transatlantic television broadcast?

818) The muscle of what organ continuously contracts, causing it to quiver 30 to 60 times per second?

819) What is note-worthy about the Tacoma Narrows Bridge?

820) What is a flat, broad-bodied, odorous insect?

821) What is the oldest and most common sedative?

822) There are 150,000 cubic miles of water beneath what desert?

823) If an electronic circuit operates in 10 nanoseconds, how many operations does it perform in a second?

. . . Answers

813. Japanese spider crab

814. It was the first manned landing on the moon.

815. Larynx

816. Alaska

817. Telstar I

818. The eye

819. It collapsed as a result of wind-driven resonance.

820. Stinkbug

821. Alcohol

822. Sahara

823. 100 million

824) This chemical element was named after the Greek word for "hidden." A similarly-named substance is Superman's weakness. What is it?

825) What is a deep blue, semi-precious stone prized by the Egyptians for its beauty?

826) What is a poisonous alkaloid extracted from tobacco leaves and widely used as an insecticide?

827) What herb yields digitalis?

828) Haliaeetus leucocephalus refers to:
    a. golden eagle
    b. bald eagle
    c. Australian wedge-tailed eagle
    d. lesser eagle

829) Tailor's chalk and soapstone are varieties of which mineral:
    a. mica
    b. talc
    c. graphite
    d. feldspar

830) What scientist obtained valuable data for his (r)evolutionary work from the Galapagos finches?

831) How many bits are in a byte?

. . . Answers

824. Krypton

825. Lapis lazuli

826. Nicotine

827. Foxglove

828. b

829. b

830. Charles Darwin

831. Eight

832) True or false: Deposits of iron in the lining of the human nose as well as in bees, birds, and dolphins may act like a magnetic compass.

833) Whose famous 4,000-year-old remains were found in China?

834) Dry ice is the frozen phase of what gas?

835) There are 206 of these in the human body. What are they?

836) What is another name for the Paleolithic Age?

837) What is a fly-catching bird which frequently calls its own name?

838) Death cap poisoning results from what?

839) What planet was discovered by Clyde Tombaugh in 1930?

840) What does a protractor measure?

841) True or false: One hundred eighty million iron atoms side by side would extend further than an inch.

842) What has 27 parts and 42.3 quintillion possible combinations?

. . . *Answers*

832. True

833. Peking Man

834. Carbon dioxide

835. Bones

836. The Stone Age

837. Phoebe

838. Eating the death cap mushroom

839. Pluto

840. Angles

841. False

842. Rubik's Cube (TM)

QUESTIONS

843) What marsupial mammals do some people espouse eating more of?

844) Binocular is to two eyes as binaural is to what?

845) What whale has teeth?

846) What three elements besides iron make up the alloy alnico, used for making magnets?

847) Lowering cholesterol intake decreases the risk of what disease?

848) Where could you observe the aurora australis?

849) Where is the largest radio telescope dish in the world?

850) What is Maryland's state bird?

IDENTITIES OF RAYS AND PARTICLES:

851) Alpha   a. Electrons

852) Beta   b. Photons

853) Gamma   c. Helium nuclei

854) True or false: A meter is longer than a yard.

. . . Answers

843. Opossum

844. Two ears

845. Sperm whale

846. Aluminum, nickel, and cobalt

847. Heart disease

848. At the south pole

849. Arecibo, Puerto Rico

850. Baltimore oriole

851. c

852. a

853. b

854. True

855) True or false: Albert Einstein was involved in the discovery of the 99th element, Einsteinium.

856) True or false: The average hummingbird weighs less than a penny.

857) Telophase is the final state of what process?

858) Deuterium and Tritium are isotopes of what element?

859) What are the flat fish whose eyes gradually migrate to one side of its head?

860) What is the product of the collision between matter and an equivalent amount of antimatter?

861) What mechanical and electronic device has a name derived from a Czechoslovakian word meaning "work, compulsory service"?

862) The Wasserman test detects the presence of:
     a. smallpox
     b. syphilis
     c. anthrax
     d. rabies

863) It took Verne's Phileas Fogg 80 days, but Yuri Gagarin did it in under two hours. What is it?

. . . *Answers*

855. False

856. True

857. Cell division (mitosis)

858. Hydrogen

859. Flounder

860. Energy

861. Robot

862. b

863. Circumnavigation of the Earth

864) What are the Geminids, the Perseids, and the Leonids?

865) What substance is secreted by the tear glands of mammals:
    a. cellulose
    b. glycogen
    c. lachrymal fluid
    d. phosphic acid

866) What is 12 days for a finch and 79 days for an albatross?

867) What were originally named "Wanderers" because of their motion thru the sky?

868) Which bird with an uncanny mimicking ability is the state bird of 5 states?

869) The poppy is which state's state flower?

870) Who first showed that full color pictures can be formed from only two single-color images?

871) What type of whale was Moby Dick?

872) If a mother with O-type blood has a B-type baby, the father cannot be:
    a. O-type
    b. B-type
    c. AB-type

. . . *Answers*

864. Meteor showers

865. c

866. The incubation period

867. Planets

868. Mockingbird

869. California

870. James H. Land

871. Sperm whale

872. a

873) What has been called "the light of the 21st century"?

874) What is the name of the temperature and pressure conditions at which water can be in the solid, liquid, and gas phases simultaneously?

875) True or false: Flamingoes get their color from blue-green algae they eat which turns pink during digestion.

876) What insects communicate with each other by distinctive dances?

877) What is the name for steel alloyed with chromium?

878) Which of the countries Yugoslavia, Cuba, and Viet Nam has not had a Cosmonaut in space?

879) What exploded on Bikini Island in 1954 and shook the world?

880) Besides adenine and thymine, what are the other two bases in DNA?

881) True or false: Parchment was made from the skins of calves, goats, and sheep.

882) What results from applying 100,000 atmospheres of pressure at 2500 degrees C to graphite?

. . . *Answers*

873. The laser

874. The triple point

875. True

876. Bees

877. Stainless steel

878. Yugoslavia

879. The first H-bomb

880. Guanine and cytosine

881. True

882. Diamond

883) What is the name of the whirling machines whose functions range from separating liquids to simulating massive gravitational accelerations?

884) True or false: Green is the longest visible wavelength of light.

885) True or false: Bald eagles are generally bald.

886) How long do red blood cells live?

887) What frequently occurs where the North American Plate meets the Pacific Plate?

888) What are "cool" areas on the surface of the Sun called?

889) Another name for rock salt is:
    a. perlite
    b. pyrite
    c. halite
    d. fluorite

890) With what is the expression "Kings play chess on fiber glass stools" associated?

891) What is a soft, sweet Chinese nut?

. . . *Answers*

883. Centrifuge

884. False

885. False

886. 120 days

887. Earthquakes

888. Sun spots

889. c

890. A mnemonic for the taxonomic categories: Kingdom, phyllum, class, order, family, genus, species

891. Lychee

892) Which one of these does not belong as a unit of force:
   a. dyne
   b. Newton
   c. pound
   d. erg

893) Hyperopia refers to what eye condition?

894) What loses over 4 tons of weight each second?

895) What is the name denoting plants that seasonally shed all their leaves?

896) What does "Homo sapiens" mean?

897) What are the only birds which migrate by swimming?

898) What musical instrument's name means "soft and loud"?

899) Angstroms, fermis, and parsecs are all measures of what?

900) True or false: Hens have to be impregnated to lay eggs.

901) What mammal is called 'the unicorn of the sea'?

. . . Answers

892. d

893. Far-sightedness

894. The Sun

895. Deciduous

896. Man of knowledge

897. Penguins

898. Piano(forte)

899. Distance

900. False

901. Narwhal

QUESTIONS

902) What substance found in bogs is the oldest fossil fuel used by man?

903) Which is the only moon in the solar system with a substantial atmosphere?

904) Glucose, fructose, and galactose are better known as what?

905) What is important about the Holocene epoch?

906) What jellyfish can induce a sting worse than a nestful of wasps?

907) What fraction of our lives is spent awake?

908) What nocturnal animal makes up one-fourth of all mammal species?

909) Is the Tropic of Cancer north or south of the equator?

910) True or false: When viewed from the North Star, all planets move clockwise around the Sun.

911) In the 1850's, Bessemer set up a factory in Sheffield to produce what?

912) Which bird doesn't know the words?

. . . Answers

902. Peat

903. Saturn's Titan

904. Sugars

905. It is our current geological epoch

906. Portuguese Man-of-War

907. Two-thirds

908. Bats

909. North

910. False

911. Steel

912. Hummingbird

913) What is another name for the semi-precious stone heliotrope?

914) What textile dye gives blue jeans their color?

915) From what part of the body of a sperm whale is sperm oil obtained?

916) True or false: Hot water freezes faster than the same amount of cold water.

917) What is the name of the whale that has a long protuding tusk?

918) What is the fatty deposit from the intestine of the whale, called ambergris, used for?

919) What part of the wooly mammoth was 16 feet long?

920) What are the four pointed teeth between the incisors and the biscuspids?

921) Osteoporosis is caused by the lack of what mineral in the body?

922) What is a googol?

923) Where are the islands of Langerhans located?

924) What is Pangea?

. . . Answers

913. Bloodstone

914. Indigo

915. The head

916. True

917. Narwhal

918. Perfume

919. Its tusks

920. Canine teeth

921. Calcium

922. Ten to the one hundredth power (1 followed by 100 zeroes)

923. In the pancreas

924. A prehistoric super-continent

QUESTIONS

925) True or false: A bacterium that divides to produce two bacteria every hour would produce more of its kind in two days than the total human population.

926) The external respiratory organs of most aquatic animals are:
   a. gills
   b. flanges
   c. dibeales
   d. staves

927) How frequently is a complete, new image formed on a U.S. television screen?

928) True or false: Monozygotic twins are not always identical.

929) True or false: Fewer than a million kinds of molecules are known.

930) What is the common name for Lysergic acid diethylamide?

931) True or false: An XY egg cell is that of a female.

932) How much force does a 100 lb. barbell exert on the Earth?

. . . Answers

925. True

926. a

927. Thirty times each second

928. False

929. True

930. LSD

931. False

932. 100 lb

933) What rare metal melts at 86 degrees F. and would turn to liquid in your hand?

934) What is 1/3 + 1/2?

935) What chemical element whose name means "light-bearing" burns spontaneously in air?

936) Who is Dr. Denton Cooley?

937) True or false: Los Angeles and San Francisco are moving toward each other at a rate of 2.5 inches per year.

938) Compact stellar sources of pulsing radio emissions are called what?

939) Which does not belong to the group of elementary particle detectors:
    a. bubble chamber
    b. cloud chamber
    c. ionization chamber
    d. they all belong

940) What has a wing-spread wider than a DC-9 but weighs less than 70 pounds?

941) An oncogene is a gene which promotes the growth of what?

. . . *Answers*

933. Gallium

934. 5/6

935. Phosphorus

936. He performed the first successful human heart transplant in the U.S.

937. True

938. Pulsars

939. d

940. The Gossamer Condor

941. Cancer (tumors)

942) Supercomputers today are able to perform how many operations per second:
    a. nearly 1 million
    b. 10 million
    c. more than 100 million.

943) True or false: Antideuteron, as an example of anti-matter, has been created in a laboratory.

944) Which bird is the state bird of seven states?

945) The nest in bird nest soup is made from what?

946) True or false: The sea anemone is a flowery ocean plant.

947) True or false: One dinosaur, Stenonychosaurus inequalus, had a brain large enough to equal that of early mammals.

948) True or false: John Glenn's first space flight cost about two cents of the average American taxpayer's taxes.

949) What is the name of decaying organic matter found on a forest floor?

950) What current farming method is used in the jungle where the vegetation is cut and set afire so the ashes will fertilize the soil?

. . . *Answers*

942. c

943. True

944. Cardinal

945. Saliva from the mouth of the male swiftlet

946. False

947. True

948. True

949. Duff

950. Slash and burn

QUESTIONS

MATH AND SCIENCE POSSESSIVES:

951) Heimlich's   a. cycle

952) Rubik's   b. equations

953) Archimedes'   c. bones

954) Napier's   d. maneuver

955) Pascal's   e. screw

956) Krebs'   f. cube

957) Maxwell's   g. triangle

958) In what ordinary device is a cathode ray tube found?

959) In what phenomenon whose name means "failure" does one heavenly body pass behind another?

960) The "iconoscope" was followed by the "image orthicon" which is an early form of what?

961) What process is the source of a firefly's light?

962) What are the Galilean satellites?

963) What is a breed of black and white cows?

. . . Answers

951. d

952. f

953. e

954. c

955. g

956. a

957. b

958. Television

959. Eclipse

960. Television camera

961. Phosphorescence

962. Four largest moons of Jupiter

963. Holstein

964) What is unusual about the daily rotation of Venus and Uranus?

965) What is the name for the bending of light rays as performed by lenses?

966) The mass of a nickel is about:
   a. 1 gram
   b. 5 grams
   c. 50 grams
   d. 500 grams

967) What is a food made from the livers of artificially-fattened geese?

968) Where on the earth are you the farthest from its center?

969) Laika, the first living creature to orbit the earth, was what type of animal?

970) What is the common name of the spiral galaxy containing our Sun?

971) What monk determined the way that traits were passed from one generation to the next in his pea garden?

972) To what do the following rules pertain: One inch — keep off; two inches — one may; three inches — small groups; four inches — okay.

. . . Answers

964. It is retrograde

965. Refraction

966. b

967. Pate de foie gras

968. At the equator

969. Dog

970. Milky Way

971. Gregor Mendel

972. Ice thickness

QUESTIONS

973) Columbian, chemical element number 41, is now officially called by what name derived from Niobe, daughter of Tantalus?

974) True or false: Ninety percent of all species that have become extinct have been birds.

975) What are the teeth at the back of the mouth?

976) What would be 33 feet tall if it were filled with water instead of mercury?

977) What element is the "new twin" whose sibling is Praseodymium meaning the "green twin"?

978) True or false: A comet's apparent size decreases as it gets closer to the Sun.

979) True or false: The lens of the eye grows with age, however its ability to focus for near vision is reduced.

980) True or false: Cerenkov counters measure particles traveling faster than the speed of light.

981) True or false: A fly's central nervous system overloads, immobilizing it when more than one threat is present.

982) What is the name of the plane figure with four sides, only two of which are parallel?

. . . Answers

973. Niobium

974. True

975. Molars

976. A barometer

977. Neodymium

978. False

979. True

980. True

981. True

982. Trapezoid

983) How many time zones are there on Earth?

984) Which rodents' mass movements sometimes result in suicide?

985) True or false: A solar eclipse may last more than eight minutes.

986) What is the name of the biochemical cycle reactions starting with lactic acid and ending with carbon dioxide and water?

987) As the weight of a pendulum's bob gets lighter, how does the pendulum's period change?

988) Millions of trees are accidentally planted each year by what animal?

989) What is the toughest and strongest human tendon, named for a Greek hero?

990) True or false: A black widow spider's venom is not as strong in early summer as at other times.

991) What is the more common name for frequency modulated broadcast?

992) What land mammal holds the record for the greatest age?

993) Besides being the second closest to the Sun, what is significant about Barnard's star?

. . . Answers

983. Twenty four

984. Lemmings

985. False

986. Krebs cycle

987. It doesn't

988. Squirrel

989. Achilles tendon

990. True

991. FM radio

992. Man

993. It is known to have a planetary system

994) True or false: The sunshine vitamin is Vitamin D.

995) Which state is in both the Western and Eastern Hemispheres?

996) Fibrous proteins provide the structural framework for animals just as what substance does for plants?

997) What animal's horn is said to be an aphrodisiac?

998) True or false: The Hevea brasiliensis tree provides latex or rubber.

999) The race of tigers that is the largest is:
   a. Sumatran
   b. Caspian
   c. Manchurian
   d. Telurian

1000) What is the most abundant tree-dwelling mammal in South America which neither sees nor hears well, almost never stands or walks, and spends most of its time sleeping upside-down?

1001) Where do you find a corona:
   a. The Sun
   b. The Eye
   c. A Car

. . . Answers

994. True

995. Alaska

996. Cellulose

997. Rhinoceros

998. True

999. c

1000. Three Toed Sloth

1001. a

MORE EXCITING READING
IN THE ZEBRA/OMNI SERIES

SENSATIONAL SAGAS!

WHITE NIGHTS, RED DAWN   (1277, $3.95)
by Frederick Nolan
Just as Tatiana was blossoming into womanhood, the Russian
Revolution was overtaking the land. How could the stunning
aristocrat sacrifice her life, her heart and her love for a cause she
had not chosen? Somehow, she would prevail over the red dawn
—and carve a destiny all her own!

IMPERIAL WINDS   (1324, $3.95)
by Priscilla Napier
From the icebound Moscow river to the misty towers of the
Kremlin, from the Bolshevick uprising to the fall of the
Romanovs, Daisy grew into a captivating woman who would
courageously fight to escape the turmoil of the raging IM-
PERIAL WINDS.

KEEPING SECRETS   (1291, $3.75)
by Suzanne Morris
It was 1914, the winds of war were sweeping the globe, and Elec-
tra was in the eye of the hurricane—rushing headlong into a mar-
riage with the wealthy Emory Cabot. Her days became a carousel
of European dignitaries, rich investors, and worldly politicians.
And her nights were filled with mystery and passion . . . .